BUILDING
WORLD LANDMARKS

The
Panama
Canal

by Scott Ingram

BLACKBIRCH®
PRESS

THOMSON

GALE

San Diego • Detroit • New York • San Francisco • Cleveland • New Haven, Conn. • Waterville, Maine • London • Munich

For more information, contact
The Gale Group, Inc.
27500 Drake Rd.
Farmington Hills, MI 48331-3535
Or you can visit our Internet site at http://www.gale.com

LIBRARY OF CONGRESS CATALOGING-IN-PUBLICATION DATA

Ingram, Scott (William Scott)
  The Panama Canal / by Scott Ingram.
    p. cm. — (Building world landmarks)
  Includes bibliographical references and index.
    ISBN 1-56711-332-X (hardback : alk. paper)
    1. Panama Canal (Panama)—History—Juvenile literature. I. Title. II.
Series.

  F1569.C2I64 2004
  972.87'5—dc21

                                                    2003004211

Printed in the United States
10 9 8 7 6 5 4 3 2 1

Table of Contents

A Construction Challenge

A CLOSE LOOK at a map of the Western Hemisphere shows why the small, S-shaped Isthmus of Panama is significant. The isthmus is a narrow strip of land that connects two larger land masses—the continents of North and South America. It is apparent from the map that being able to cross the isthmus creates a shortcut around the southern tip of South America in a journey between the Atlantic and Pacific Oceans. That is why the isthmus has always been an important geographical location, and it is why the Panama Canal was built there.

The construction of the canal, however, was much more difficult than it appears on a map. Connecting the two oceans required men to move mountains and build dams. It required builders to create lakes and lay down railroad tracks. Machines and materials had to be brought to the tropical jungles from thousands of

Opposite:
Photographed from space, the Panama Canal appears as a brown river cutting across the Isthmus of Panama and connecting the Pacific (left) and Atlantic (upper right corner) Oceans.

By using the fifty-mile-long Panama Canal, these ships shorten their trips by thousands of miles. More than fourteen thousand vessels use the canal every year.

miles away. The construction of the Panama Canal also cost the lives of thousands of workers.

Today, more than fourteen thousand ships a year make the fifty-mile (eighty-five kilometer) passage through the canal. The eight- to ten-hour trip can shorten the journey of a vessel traveling around the tip of South America by thousands of miles. Since the Panama Canal opened in 1914, nearly 1 million ships have traveled through what historians agree is one of the great engineering marvels of the modern world.

Canals and Locks

In ancient times, before rail lines or paved roads, travel by boat was the most efficient way to move goods and people over long distances. Rivers, lakes, and oceans were the highways of the ancient world. In areas where natural waterways existed, canals were dug in order to connect them.

The oldest and longest canal in the world is the Grand Canal of China. Built between 400 B.C. and A.D. 600, the canal is more than eleven hundred miles long. Still in use today, it is crossed by more than sixty bridges. Because of its great length, builders faced a common problem—raising and lowering boats to accommodate changes in elevation. To accomplish this, the Chinese developed a device that is still used today—the lock.

A canal lock is essentially a large enclosure that opens at two ends. When a vessel must be moved from a high water level to a lower one, the gate at the low end is kept closed. Water is let in from the higher level lock until the depth is equal to the water level of the upper lock. At that point, the upper lock gate between the two opens and the vessel

Boats line up in one of the locks of China's Grand Canal. Invented by the Chinese, locks help boats move forward when water levels change.

enters the lock. Next, the upper gate is closed, the lower gate is opened to allow water out, and the boat continues on its way. To move up a level, the process is reversed.

The number of locks in a canal depends on the change in elevation. In the 363 miles of the Erie Canal, for example, there are eighty-three locks. In a canal such as the one hundred-mile Suez, which is at sea level for its entire length, there are no locks.

Chapter 1

Beginnings

LONG BEFORE THE Panama Canal was built, explorers understood the importance of the Isthmus of Panama. In 1501, the first Europeans sailed into the area. They were led by Christopher Columbus and landed at several points on the northern coast of the isthmus during his fourth voyage to the Americas. In 1511, the first Spanish expedition landed in an area known to the natives as Panama, which meant "many fish" in their language.

During that expedition, the Spaniards, under the command of Vasco Núñez de Balboa and Francisco Pizarro, established the settlement of Darien. The settlement, which eventually grew to more than two thousand Spaniards, was built over a destroyed Indian village that was ransacked by the Spaniards after they saw gold ornaments worn by the natives there. This first permanent European settlement on the North

Opposite:
Ruins from the first Spanish settlement in the Americas still stand today in Panama.

This painting depicts Vasco Núñez de Balboa as he views the Pacific Ocean in 1513. Balboa, along with Francisco Pizarro, established the first European settlement in Panama.

and South American continents was located at the narrow strip of land between the two land masses.

In the first two years of settlement, the Spaniards were able to subdue natives in the area. During that time, they heard many stories from natives of a large body of water across the jungle—an ocean that the Spaniards did not know existed. In 1513, Balboa and Pizarro set off with a force of two hundred to find the body of water. The Spaniards slowly made their way in intense humidity through dense rain forests, steep mountains, and thick clouds of mosquitoes. On September 29, 1513, while Pizarro watched from the shore, Balboa waded into the waters of the Pacific Ocean, which he named the Sea of the South.

Spain's Empire Rises and Falls

The discovery of an unknown ocean drew more explorers to the region. During the next twenty years, Spanish settlements were established on both the Atlantic and Pacific coasts of Panama, and Spain gained control of much of Central and South America. During that time, Spanish explorers led by Pizarro captured large amounts of gold in battles with the Inca empire in Peru. There was so much of the valuable metal that

Francisco Pizarro led Spanish armies across Central and South America to look for gold. He and his men carried stolen gold from Peru across the Camino Real to waiting Spanish ships on the east coast.

within a few years, Spain had become the wealthiest nation on Earth. Transporting the treasure across the isthmus on the backs of mules and native slaves, however, resulted in a great loss of life—and gold. The most difficult part of the journey back to Spain became the trip through the thick, mosquito-infested, rain-soaked jungle.

By the 1530s, a primitive roadway seven feet wide had been chopped through the dense undergrowth of the isthmus and paved with cobblestones. This path, called the Camino Real, which means King's Highway, was used to transport gold to Spanish ships anchored on the Atlantic coast of Panama.

In 1534, in an attempt to ease the trip across the isthmus, King Charles I of Spain ordered Panama to be surveyed to determine the best place to construct a canal. Although a route was chosen, the difficulty of excavating the waterway through jungle swamps and across powerful rivers proved too challenging, and the idea was forgotten.

Over the next century, the Isthmus of Panama was an important location in the Spanish empire. It served as the main landing area for expeditions into South and Central America. The presence of treasure-laden ships, however, brought pirates as well as naval vessels from Spain's enemy, England, to the Atlantic coast. In the seventeenth and early eighteenth centuries, transport ships anchored in wealthy ports became frequent targets of raiders. Those conflicts made Panama a dangerous destination, and once most of the gold had been removed from the region,

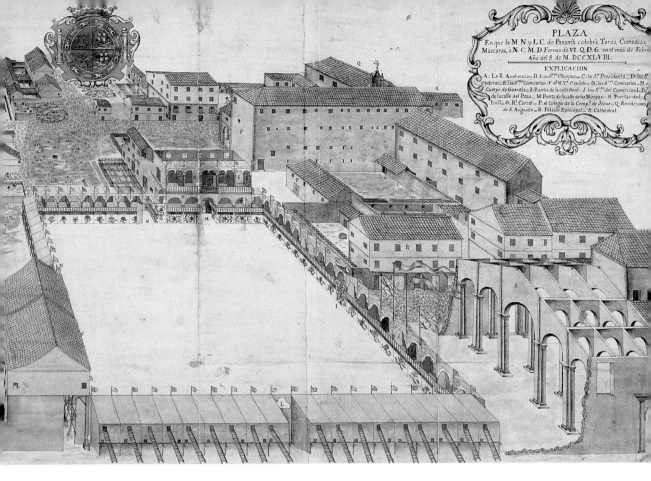

colonists and explorers went to more secure Spanish settlements in Mexico and South America.

In the early 1800s, Central and South American colonists revolted against Spanish rule. Within ten years, the former colonies became independent nations. In 1821, the colony of Panama became a district of the country of Colombia.

A Second Look at Panama

The Colombian Isthmus of Panama remained largely unsettled until the expansion of the United States. By the 1830s, Americans had begun to cross the Great Plains and the Rocky Mountains on their way to Oregon and

This eighteenth-century painting of Panama City shows the city's grand plaza in the center. Panama became part of Colombia in 1821.

Geography and Climate of the Isthmus

The Isthmus of Panama is shaped like the letter S and is located between five hundred and seven hundred miles north of the equator. To its east is Colombia and to its west is Costa Rica. The position of the isthmus can lead to unexpected compass directions. A vessel crossing the Panama Canal from the Pacific to the Atlantic, for example, does not travel west to east—instead it travels southeast to northwest. The sunrise over the canal is to the east over the Pacific Ocean and sets to the west in the Atlantic.

The main landform obstacle for the canal builders was the spine of a mountain range called the Cordillera Central Panama, which runs through the center of Panama and rises about nine hundred feet above sea level. This range was formed as the result of volcanic activity, and in the fifty miles across the isthmus there are five major volcanic cores that have caused numerous faults, or breaks, in the surface. The mountains are where the sources of most of the five hundred rivers that flow through Panama are located. Fewer than twenty of the rivers are suitable for

The Cordillera Central Panama, a rain-forested mountain range, was a major obstacle to building a canal across the isthmus.

boats because of rapids and steep drops. The majority are fast flowing and deep due to the high rainfall in the region. Panama's longest river, the Chagres, was dammed to create Gatun Lake, a major segment of the canal's route.

The isthmus region has a very humid, tropical climate with daily temperatures that range from eighty to ninety degrees Fahrenheit. Rainfall in Panama ranges from one hundred to two hundred inches per year, most of which falls in the rainy season between April and November.

the Mexican territory of California. This overland journey took many months and was filled with danger. The only other way to reach the West Coast was by ship around the tip of South America, a journey that was much longer, more costly, and equally dangerous. For these reasons, Panama was once again examined as an alternate route.

In 1835, Charles Biddle, a colonel in the U.S. Army, was sent to Panama to evaluate the possibility of constructing a canal. By that time, many canals were in use in the United States, including the 363-mile Erie Canal, which had been completed ten years earlier. Biddle was only in the rain forest for four days, however, before he declared that building a canal across the isthmus was impossible.

Impossible or not, the need for a shortcut to the West increased in the late 1840s. In 1848, California became a U.S. territory after the American victory in a war with Mexico. That same year, gold was discovered in the mountains east of Sacramento, and the territory soon became a U.S. state. Suddenly, there was an enormous demand for transportation to the West Coast. That demand focused the attention of businessmen on the isthmus in hopes of making money by transporting eager gold seekers to California.

The Panama Railroad

By the late 1840s, canals had become obsolete because of the development of railroads, which provided faster travel. In 1849, a group of U.S. businessmen formed the Panama Railroad Company. The Americans paid the

Colombian government a large fee for the right to construct a railroad across the Isthmus of Panama. Work began in May 1850, and the plans called for a fifty-mile rail line to follow a route similar to the one that had been surveyed by the Spanish three centuries earlier.

Company owners told investors that the rail line across the isthmus could be built in six months at a cost of about a million dollars. At the time, it was not unusual for laborers in the United States to lay two to three miles of track a day. A fifty-mile connection between the oceans seemed relatively simple—on paper.

Almost immediately, however, the differences between building a railroad in the United States and building one in a swamp-filled rain forest became obvious. For example, the engineers had surveyed the route during its brief dry season. When work began, the wet season arrived, bringing with it more than seven months of drenching rain. Workers sank neck deep in muck, and heavy equipment disappeared into mud 150 feet deep. Thousands of tons of "spoil" —excavated rock and soil—had to be removed by hand, transported, and dumped into the swamps to make the land solid enough to support tracks.

Work was also held up for another reason. The swamps were infested with large numbers of mosquitoes. Thousands of workers, mainly poor immigrants from Europe and Asia, died from diseases such as malaria and yellow fever, which insects had transmitted to them. The deadly combination of the wet season and disease severely delayed the project; after twenty months, less than seven miles of track had been laid.

In 1855, five years after it was begun, the Panama Railroad was completed. It had cost ten times the original estimate—and taken ten times longer to build than had been planned. In addition to filling in swamps, more than three hundred bridges had to be built to carry trains over rivers and valleys. It is estimated that ten thousand to fifteen thousand lives were lost in the construction.

This print shows the western end of the Panama Railroad, completed in 1855.

The French Attempt and the American Plan

BY THE TIME the railroad opened, the California gold rush had essentially come to an end. Nevertheless, the Panama Railroad still served as the main connection between the Atlantic and Pacific coasts. In 1869, the transcontinental railroad across the United States was completed, and the Panama Railroad was soon forgotten. The dream of a canal across the isthmus, however, remained alive.

The idea of bringing the Panama Canal to reality arose in 1869. That year, another important canal construction project on the opposite side of the world from Panama and the United States was completed. The Suez Canal, which connected the Mediterranean and the Red Seas, was opened. The main director of the one hundred-mile canal project was a French businessman, Ferdinand-Marie de Lesseps. To raise money for the Suez Canal, Lesseps had persuaded

Opposite:
A cargo ship chugs along the completed Panama Canal. From the Spanish discovery of the isthmus in the 1500s until the twentieth century, several attempts to build a canal across Panama failed.

wealthy Europeans to invest in the project—and the investors were handsomely rewarded.

The French Canal Company

Lesseps saw an opportunity to again enrich investors by putting his canal-building experience to use in Panama. In the 1870s, Lesseps formed a company and developed plans for a Panama canal. At the same time, he negotiated with the Colombian government for the land-use rights to build the canal. In 1879, with negotiations settled, Lesseps bought the Panama Railroad to build his canal. He wanted to use the rails to move equipment and remove spoil during the excavation.

Frenchman Ferdinand-Marie de Lesseps promoted the building of the Suez and Panama Canals. He succeeded with the Suez Canal but gave up on the Panama Canal.

20

Lesseps, however, was not an engineer, and the excavation plan he developed was based on the work done at the Suez Canal. The canal designed for the isthmus was to be built at sea level across the entire route. There would be no locks, devices for raising and lowering ships, as there were on most canals with varying elevations. The mountains that rose in the middle of the isthmus would be demolished, according to Lesseps, with dynamite, a powerful explosive that had been invented in 1866.

The fact that the Panama Canal was just half the length of the Suez Canal made Lesseps confident that his plan could be accomplished. If his engineers encountered problems, Lesseps told his investors, "men of genius will step forward to solve them, [and] science will find a way."

The Wet Season

Science, however, had no answer for the climate of Panama. The difference between the flat, dry desert at Suez and the swampy conditions of the isthmus were enormous. Like the U.S. railroad engineers thirty years earlier, Lesseps visited Panama in the dry season to plan his canal. Again, once the rains began, workers battled mud and landslides. Mosquitoes were so thick, complained one worker, that "you get a mouthful with every breath." The attempted excavation was made even more difficult by the fact that the Chagres River crossed the planned path of the canal fourteen times. As the rains continued day after day, some workers were swept away in dam collapses and others were

This painting shows a riot by French workers who refused to work on the Panama Canal because of the horrible conditions.

buried under mud from rain-soaked hillsides that gave way. After six years, less than 10 percent of the planned excavation was complete.

The delay cost both lives and money. In 1889, Lesseps declared bankruptcy with only eleven miles of the canal excavated. Investors lost millions of dollars, and Lesseps was tried and sentenced to five years in prison for fraud. More than twenty-seven thousand workers had died in ten years. In the final months of the project, a newspaper editorial headline asked "Is de Lesseps a Canal Digger or a Grave Digger?"

For several years after the end of the French project, the canal was forgotten. Interest revived during the Spanish-American War in 1898. During that brief conflict, which was fought largely in Cuba, the battleship USS *Oregon* was ordered from its home port in San Francisco to the Caribbean Sea. The voyage around the tip of South America took sixty-seven days, and by the time the ship arrived, the war was almost over. The secretary of the U.S. Navy, Theodore Roosevelt, knew that for the navy to be effective, its ships would have to be able to travel more quickly.

The American Plan

Roosevelt's frustration with the slow travel of naval ships did not last long. In 1901, Roosevelt, who had become vice president, became president when William McKinley was assassinated. Roosevelt immediately took action to build a canal across the Isthmus of Panama. Unlike the French attempt, however, this project had the support of a government rather than a private company.

In 1902, the United States paid $40 million to the French canal company for the right to use its canal land and abandoned equipment. The property the company sold the rights to, however, had been leased from Colombia. When Colombia's leaders learned that the U.S. government planned to construct a canal in their territory, they refused to permit the transfer of the land lease.

Roosevelt was enraged that Colombia decided to treat the American government differently from a private French company. After several failed attempts to reach an agreement, he put U.S. support behind a rebel movement in Panama that demanded independence from Colombia. Roosevelt ordered U.S. battleships to anchor off both coasts of Panama to prevent Colombia from landing troops to fight the Panamanian rebels. With the powerful naval support of the United States, the new nation of Panama was founded in 1902.

In return for Roosevelt's help in securing Panama's independence, the new nation's leaders agreed to a land-use treaty with the United States. In 1903, the United States paid $10 million to lease a ten-mile-wide strip of land across the isthmus and to obtain the right to build a canal there. The land became an American territory, and canal workers arrived in late 1903.

"A Fit Place to Live"

The problems faced by the American work crews in the new U.S. territory in 1903 were the same as those faced by Lesseps's force in the previous century: rain and disease. To make matters worse, the chief engineer of the project, John Wallace, failed to arrange for sufficient food to be delivered. Living conditions were filthy and disease spread almost immediately. Three out of every four American workers left Panama during the first year. Among them was Wallace, who was fired.

Wallace was replaced by John Stevens, a civil engineer who had many years of experience in railroad construction. He decided that before the canal could be built, worker conditions had to be improved, so he ordered his men to make the Canal Zone "a fit place to live." Running water and sewage pipes were laid, and arrangements were made for fresh food to be shipped to Panama regularly. Also, Canal Zone land was set aside for farms to provide fruits, vegetables, milk, and eggs.

Panama Money

Although the Panama Canal was planned and built by the U.S. government, most of the actual labor was provided by workers from various countries in the West Indies. Between 1904 and 1914, black workers from Barbados, Jamaica, and Martinique made up two-thirds of the canal's labor force—a total of more than twenty-five thousand laborers.

In the early twentieth century, these island nations were extremely poor and unemployment was high. Because of this, their governments allowed the United States to recruit workers from their countries. The result was a flood of young men, eager to earn the relatively high wages: ten cents an hour. In Barbados, between 30 and 40 percent of all adult men went to Panama to work. The largest recruitment of men took place in 1907, when nearly fifteen thousand workers came to the isthmus.

Because there was little to do but work and rest, many workers were able to send their wages home. During the years of construction, some workers accumulated a great deal of what became known as Panama money. After the

Most of the workers on the Panama Canal came from the poor islands of the West Indies.

canal's completion, many workers used their savings to pay for passage to the United States. Many Americans of West Indian descent have ancestors who came to the United States with Panama money.

Not all workers, of course, were fortunate enough to leave the Canal Zone with their health and savings intact. Of more than five thousand workers killed during the building of the U.S.-led construction of the Panama Canal, more than forty-five hundred were from the West Indies.

As important as sanitary conditions and fresh food were, Stevens made the elimination of malaria and yellow fever an even bigger priority. By the early twentieth century, doctors had determined that malaria and yellow fever were carried by mosquitoes—a fact unknown only a few decades earlier. To destroy the environment in which mosquitoes bred, Stevens had workers dig ditches and small canals to drain swamps near living areas. Workers also sprayed tons of insect poisons. Soon, disease was controlled. Villages with homes, schools, churches, stores, and community halls rose in what had once been dense jungle.

Stevens's Plan

While these improvements were under way, Stevens drew up a plan for what he called a lock-and-lake

John Stevens, the second chief engineer to lead the Panama Canal project, improved living and working conditions for the building crews on the project.

canal. Instead of a sea-level waterway, Stevens wanted to construct a series of locks to raise and lower ships across the higher elevations of the isthmus. As an engineer with experience in rail construction, Stevens knew that the old French line was useless, so he built a new rail line along the existing path. This new line used heavier track and was able to carry the weight of twenty-five-car freight trains that would haul spoil from excavated areas. With the rail line in place, workers began to dig.

Although the initial excavation progressed smoothly, rain continued to disrupt the project. Landslides were a constant danger, and it was not uncommon for them to set back the work schedule for months. By 1907, the enormous pressure that Stevens had been under pushed him to mental and physical exhaustion, and he resigned his position.

This public school was built in the Canal Zone as part of the U.S. government's plan to make the zone a "fit place to live."

"One of the Great Works of the World"

JOHN STEVENS WAS replaced by Colonel George Goethals, a U.S. Army engineer who had experience in the construction of lock-type canals. In addition to his technical knowledge, Goethals, a career military man, brought a firm sense of discipline and organization to the project when he arrived in late 1907. He created a bookkeeping system to track the costs of the different materials and jobs—a practice that had never been followed in canal projects. Goethals's men worked ten hours a day, six days a weeks for top wages at that time—ten cents an hour—and work crews were scheduled far in advance for different projects to make certain that workers were busy every day. Every Sunday, Goethals personally held a complaint session at which workers could address problems on the job.

Although he came up with many innovations to make the project more efficient, Goethals followed the

Opposite:
The intricate lock system of the Panama Canal enables cargo ships to move smoothly at varying water levels.

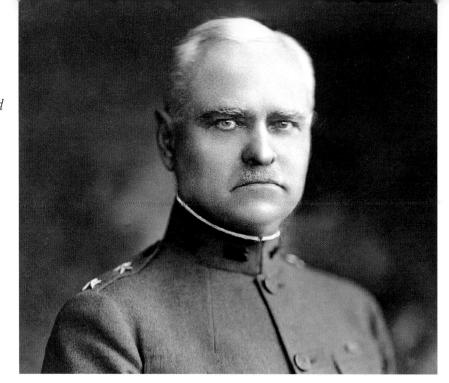

Colonel George Goethals, the third chief engineer of the Panama Canal project, directed workers as they built the canal's many locks.

plan that had been developed: Stevens's lock-lake idea. The plan was based on the construction of a dam, built from excavated spoil, which would hold back the powerful Chagres River. The river would be diverted into channels around the dam until it was complete. The dammed water would eventually form Gatun Lake, which would become what was then the world's largest artificial lake, at the canal's highest point. Ships would sail across the lake. Under the plan, the dam would use electric generators powered by the river's water to operate the locks on either end of the lake.

The lock aspect of the plan called for a total of six locks. Three locks on the Atlantic side of the isthmus would be constructed at the end of the seven-mile channel from Limon Bay. After a ship left the channel, it would begin a 1.2-mile (1.9 kilometers) transit through the three locks. During this passage, a ship would be elevated 85 feet (26 meters). The vessel then traveled 23.5 miles (37.6 kilometers) across Gatun Lake, where it would enter the fourth lock, Pedro Miguel, which lowered it 31 feet (9.4 meters). A ship would then travel 8.5 miles (13.7 kilometers) along the Culebra Cut to the 1-mile-wide (1.6 kilometers) Miraflores Lake. There the ship would enter the final two Miraflores Locks, which lowered it the final 54 feet (16.5 meters) to the level of the Pacific Ocean. The remaining 8 miles (12.8 kilometers) is a channel to the ocean.

The steel for the locks' walls, gates, and other parts was cast in Pittsburgh, Pennsylvania. In 1908, more than fifty steel mills began to make the individual parts for the canal's locks. Meanwhile, the excavation continued under Goethals's direction, with crews on the Atlantic and Pacific sides working toward the center.

A dam built across the Chagres River as part of the Panama Canal project formed Gatun Lake (pictured).

The Excavation

The most difficult section of the excavation was the 8.75 miles (14 kilometers) between the Chagres River and the Pedro Miguel Locks. This was the highest point of the isthmus and became known as the Culebra Cut, after the mountain that had to be removed for construction. The removal of the rock and hard clay that formed the mountain was performed by new and improved machines that did much of the work formerly done by hand.

One of the most useful labor-saving machines was the Lidgerwood unloader, which removed spoil from freight cars. The Lidgerwood was essentially a huge plow that was secured to the last car in the train with a long cable and linked to a winch mounted at the head of the train. The locomotive engine turned the winch, which pulled the plow forward and pushed the

This print shows the large-scale construction needed to dig the canal. At one point, the workers had to remove an entire mountain.

spoil off the cars. An unloader, operated by twenty men, could empty a twenty-car train in ten minutes—a task that once took five hundred men more than eight hours to complete by hand.

After the spoil was unloaded, the dirt spreader, another American invention, came into use. This was a single railroad car powered by compressed air with plow-shaped steel extensions on each side that could be raised and lowered like wings. The dirt spreader smoothed and leveled the material left beside the tracks by the unloader. Once the material was spread, the track shifter came into use. This huge cranelike apparatus could lift entire sections of track—rails and ties—and move them as much as nine feet. In a single day, a track shifter could move a mile of track. Because the tracks were shifted constantly as loads of spoil were spread, the machine saved enormous amounts of time.

The Spoil

Yet even with labor-saving machines, the work was difficult and dangerous. Although the number of work-related deaths was far fewer than took place during the railroad and the French canal projects in Panama, more than five thousand workers died during the lock-and-lake excavation. Mishaps with dynamite were not unusual. The worst single explosion, in 1908, killed twenty-three workers and injured forty. Like many of the accidents, it occurred in the excavation of the Culebra Cut.

The excavation work of the Culebra Cut continued for five years. Steam shovels loaded as many as 200 trainloads of rock and hard clay a day. In March 1912, the busiest month of the project, more than 3,200 trains hauled 65,500 freight cars of spoil out of the Culebra Cut alone.

Much of the spoil went to build the half-mile-thick Gatun Dam. The 1.5-mile-long (2.4 kilometers) dam was the largest earthen dam in the world at the time. A great deal of spoil was also used to connect four small islands on the Pacific side to create a breakwater that protected the canal's entrance from wave damage. As the excavation proceeded year after year, the locks were cast and shipped from the United States to the site.

The Enormous Locks

Because the canal's chief engineer, Goethals, had established precise schedules, there was no slowdown between phases of the Panama Canal project. As soon as an area for a lock was excavated, concrete was poured. In 1909, the first concrete at the canal was poured. Work with this relatively new material, however, had been done by engineers earlier.

Concrete is a mixture of sand, gravel, and cement—a powder of lime and several minerals—that is combined with water and poured into forms to harden. Before its use on the Panama Canal, concrete had been used for less than a decade—and only in dry areas such as the floors and foundations of homes. Concrete had never been used under water, and the canal's engineers were uncertain exactly what would happen to the material under the pressure and constant movement of millions of gallons of water. Tests to mix the right balance of dry

materials and water were necessary before the locks' concrete floors could be poured.

After engineers determined the right combination, the locks were poured. Each lock was 1,000 feet long and 110 feet wide. The walls of each were as high as a seven-story building. To allow for the simultaneous passage of two ships moving in either the same or opposite directions, plans called for the individual locks to be built with two chambers.

A total of six locks meant that twelve chambers had to be constructed. Enormous quantities of concrete were required for the locks. All of the cement for the concrete was shipped to Panama from New York, but the sand and gravel came from quarries

The enormous locks of the Panama Canal had walls that were seven stories high. The canal plan called for six locks to be built.

located on the isthmus. At the three Gatun Locks alone, enough concrete was poured to build a wall 1.5 feet (.5 meter) wide and 3.25 feet tall (1 meter) across the United States.

Controlling the Water

In addition to determining the size of the locks, engineers had to solve the problem of getting the water in and out of the chambers smoothly. They did this by designing the locks so that water flowed into each chamber through giant tunnels, called culverts, which were eighteen feet (5.9 meters) in diameter. The culverts carried water along the length of the chambers within the center and side walls of the locks. From these culverts, twenty smaller tubes ran beneath each chamber's floor. These crossing tubes had five openings, a total of one hundred holes in each chamber for water to flow in or out. The large number of holes permitted the even distribution of water into the chambers, which prevented boats from movements that could damage the lock's gate and doors.

Each gate door was connected by steel arms, called struts, to wheels inside a lock's walls. Each wheel in turn was linked to an electric motor, which pulled and pushed the strut back and forth to turn the wheel that moved a gate. The gates were so well balanced that only a forty-horsepower motor—about half the power of a small car engine—was needed to open and close each gate.

The final part of the lock put in place was a locomotive system that ran on tracks built on top of the

locks' walls. The locomotive filled the same role as that of a tugboat in a harbor—it guided ships as they moved through the locks so that the ships would not have to use their large engines in a small space.

The Final Steps

Even before the gates and locks were assembled, the construction of the Panama Canal was awe inspiring to many people. Roosevelt, whose frustration with the slow travel times between coasts helped lead to the canal's construction, became the first president to visit the canal site in 1906. The president was astonished at the magnitude of the operation. "This is one of the great works of the world," he said in a speech to the assembled workers as he stood in a section of the Culebra Cut.

President Theodore Roosevelt (center, in white) visited the canal site in 1906 and declared the canal "one of the great works of the world."

"A Work of Civilization"

ROOSEVELT LEFT OFFICE in 1909, long before the canal was complete. The locks on the Pacific side were finished first—Pedro Miguel in 1911 and Miraflores in 1912. On May 20, 1913, steam shovels from each side broke through the final section of the Culebra Cut, and the last cement was poured at the Gatun Locks. On June 27, 1913, the Gatun Dam was completed, and the lake rose to its full height. All that remained were a series of tests and trials to make certain all of the components of the canal were operating properly.

That testing process lasted a year and, on August 15, 1914, the USS *Ancon*, a cement transport ship, became the first vessel to cross the isthmus. The trip took nine hours and forty minutes, only a bit longer than it takes today. This event received little publicity, however, due to an event that occurred the day before when the first shots of World War I were fired in Europe.

Opposite:
Opened in the summer of 1914, the Panama Canal has allowed nearly a million ships to pass from one ocean to another in only a few hours.

Until the end of World War I in 1918, about two hundred ships per year crossed the Panama Canal. In the 1920s, the number of crossings rose to five thousand ships a year, and now about thirteen thousand ships cross the isthmus annually. During the eighty years since it was opened, the canal has undergone few repairs. The original concrete for the locks has remained solid since it was first poured. Rail tracks on the locks have been replaced to support larger tow engines. In the late twentieth century, the Galliard Cut (formerly the Culebra Cut) was widened from 530 feet (162 meters) to 630 feet (192 meters) to accommodate new, wider transport vessels and cruise ships. Oil supertankers, which are nearly 50 feet (15 meters) too wide to fit through the locks, are the only vessels that cannot fit through the canal.

The Panama Canal was widened in the late 1900s to accommodate today's larger vessels, such as this cruise ship.

Other changes to the canal involve the cost of passing through it. The first toll rate was 90 cents per ton. Today it is slightly more than $2.50 per ton, and the average toll a ship pays is about $45,000. The most common cargo from the Atlantic to the Pacific side is grain. Much of that grain comes from American farms and is headed for Asian ports. The most common cargo that passes through the canal from the Pacific to the Atlantic is cars, usually Japanese cars on transports headed for American ports in the South and East.

Whatever the cargo or the direction, passage requires that the command of each ship be handed over to a canal pilot specially trained to handle a ship through the narrow channels of the canal and the tight quarters of the locks. In most years, there have been fewer than twenty accidents among the thousands of crossings made.

The Handover

The greatest change to the canal, however, came in regard to its ownership. For more than seventy-five years, the ten-mile-wide (sixteen kilometer) Canal Zone was a territory that operated under U.S. federal laws. The zone had its own court system and police force supervised and staffed by Americans. While the canal was under U.S. control, Panamanians expressed displeasure over the presence of a foreign power within their borders. There were outbreaks of anti-American violence during the 1930s and again in the 1960s.

As a result of the unrest in Panama, the country fell under control of a series of military leaders. Political

The Panama Canal and its ten-mile-wide zone belonged to the United States until 1999, when full control of the zone was returned to Panama.

turmoil became a recurring problem, and the Canal Territory eventually became an isolated symbol of American power that created resentment in smaller, poorer nations of Central America.

In order to reduce tensions in the area, U.S. president Jimmy Carter believed that the Panama Canal had to be given to Panama. In 1977, the U.S. Congress acted on Carter's request and approved a treaty that returned gradual control of the Canal Zone and operation of the canal to Panama. That process was finalized with a ceremony in 1999. Today the canal is operated almost entirely by Panamanians.

As the Panama Canal begins its second century in operation, it is recognized by historians as one of the great engineering wonders of the modern world.

Some say that the construction of a canal across fifty miles of swamp and rain forest was as remarkable an accomplishment as putting a man on the moon. In fact, if the spoil excavated from those fifty miles was placed in railroad freight cars, the train would be long enough to circle Earth four times.

The completion of the Panama Canal established the United States as a world superpower because the nation's navy could quickly travel between oceans and mainland coasts. It was also a project that brought people from all parts of the world together to work toward one goal. Some were residents of the West Indies who used their earnings—called Panama Money—to pay their way into the United States. In connecting the world's oceans, say historians, the canal helped bring people closer. One writer described the Panama Canal as "a work of civilization."

In 1977, President Jimmy Carter (left) and General Omar Torrijos Herrera (right) announced that the United States would give the Panama Canal Zone to Panama.

Chronology

1513 Vasco Núñez de Balboa crosses the Isthmus of Panama from the Atlantic to the Pacific Oceans.

1534 King Charles I of Spain orders surveying of a canal across the isthmus, but nothing comes of the plan.

1835 The U.S. government examines the possibility of building a canal, but the idea is quickly discarded.

1855 The Panama Railroad is completed after five years, at a cost of $10 million. During construction, ten thousand to fifteen thousand workers die.

1880 A French company led by Ferdinand-Marie de Lesseps begins work on the Panama Canal.

1889 Lesseps's canal company files for bankruptcy, and work on the canal stops.

1901 President Theodore Roosevelt commits the U.S. government to building the Panama Canal.

1903 Roosevelt supports Panamanian rebels in war against Colombia with American warships. Panama secures independence from Colombia. The United States creates the Canal Zone, a territory of the United States that runs across the isthmus, in a treaty with Panama.

1904	The United States begins construction of the Panama Canal.
1905	John Stevens takes charge of Panama Canal construction and conceives the canal's lock-and-lake design. Due to dramatically improved living conditions, yellow fever is eradicated among the workers.
1906	Roosevelt visits canal work site while in office.
1907	Colonel George Goethals takes charge of Panama Canal project.
1909	Construction of locks begins.
1913	Steam shovels complete work at the Culebra Cut's excavation. Workforce totals 44,733—the largest number at any time during the project. Locks are completed.
1914	Official opening takes place on August 15. The USS *Ancon* makes the first passage in nine hours, forty minutes.
1977	President Jimmy Carter and Panamanian leader General Omar Torrijos Herrera meet to sign a treaty that will hand over U.S. control of the canal and Canal Zone to Panama on December 31, 1999.
1999	Panama takes over the canal on December 31.

Glossary

canal—an artificially created waterway

civil engineer—a person trained in the science of construction and building

concrete—building material made from sand, gravel, and cement

dense—thick or solid

estimate—a guess based on certain information

excavate—to dig out and remove

generator—a machine that produces electricity

isthmus—a narrow strip of land between two large land masses

lock—a device that raises and lowers vessels on a canal

malaria—a tropical disease spread by mosquitoes

spoil—excavated rock and dirt

survey—to measure and map out a section of land

swamp—wetland periodically covered by water

yellow fever—a tropical disease spread by mosquitoes

For More Information

Books

Lesley A. Dutemple, *The Panama Canal*. Minneapolis: Lerner, 2003.

Tim McNeese, *The Panama Canal*. San Diego: Lucent Books, 1997.

Judith St. George, *The Panama Canal: Gateway to the World*. New York: Putnam, 1989.

Barbara Winkelman, *The Panama Canal*. New York: Childrens Press, 1999.

Websites

Canal Museum (www.canalmuseum.com)
History of the canal.

How the Panama Canal Works (www.ared.com)
Excellent animation of a ship's passage.

The Panama Canal (www.pancanal.com)

Good interactive site with photographs.

TR's Legacy: The Panama Canal (www.pbs.org)
Historical review of the role of Theodore Roosevelt and the United States.

Index